The Wonders of MACA!

Carmen Mattes

I'd like to thank my kids for their support and for their hilarious sense of humor, they always keep me laughing. And a special thanks to my loving husband Jack who has supported me and believed in me in most of my endeavors.

The Wonders of MACA
by Carmen Mattes

Oceanside Publishing
119 - 17 Fawcett Road,
Coquitlam, BC
Canada V3K 6V2
www.oceansidepublishing.com

Edited by: Maureen Egan
Cover Design: Mitch Curby
Interior Design & Production: MediaWorks

ISBN 0-9735967-4-8
Printed in Canada

TABLE OF CONTENTS

Foreword

Stress of any kind causes hormonal imbalances, including higher levels of cortisol in the blood. While this may be harmless and even advantageous if it occurs on an occasional basis, high cortisol may lead to serious health problems when it becomes chronic. High blood pressure, heart attacks, strokes, adult-onset diabetes, depression, burnout, arthritis, and cancer may well be the end result of chronically elevated cortisol levels. While it is important to make diet and lifestyle changes to bring cortisol back into balance, there is a nutritional supplement that can also be a lifesaver.

I take maca on a regular basis and have done so for close to five years. As one of North America's aging baby boomers, I want to do my best to minimize the effects of stress. In this and many other regards, maca may well be the most interesting food supplement on the market.

Maca appears to be popular with both sexes. It has gained a reputation with men as a sexual and fertility enhancing food. And women looking for alternatives to potentially dangerous hormone prescriptions have also found maca to be extremely valuable.

Hot flashes, osteoporosis, insomnia, memory loss, severe mood swings, and easy weight gain are just some of the more annoying things that happen to women during the so-called "change of life." In men, the low DHEA and testosterone levels that cause depression, low libido, and erectile dysfunction are increasingly being recognized as factors in a similar condition termed andropause. If you are looking for a single supplement to make the menopause or andropause more enjoyable (or more tolerable), maca should definitely be considered.

Aside from mid-life changes, maca has numerous other benefits including a boost in stamina, better athletic performance without steroids, disease prevention, and immune system enhancement at any age. It is virtually side-effect free and is safe for both pregnant women and infants. Why all this is so is the subject of this book.

What's the best way to take maca? Is one brand better than another? And how can you tell? How does maca work as an energy booster as well as an anxiety reducer? Is maca a stimulant like ephedra? The story of maca, its supporting scientific documentation, and practically anything you ever wanted to know about how, where, when, and why to use it are very well described by Carmen Mattes. May you forever be stress free as a result of reading her book.

Zoltan P. Rona, MD, MSc
Author & Medical Editor,
Encyclopedia of Natural Healing
(Alive Books, 2002)

Preface

I was seventeen years old when I first became interested in natural health, herbs, and vitamins. One of the first books I picked up and read was *Let's Eat Right to Keep Fit,* by Adelle Davis. In fact, that book still sits proudly on my shelf.

As I read paragraph after page after chapter, I just knew that I needed every single vitamin and mineral Adelle spoke of, and I needed them all NOW! Every morning I ate a handful of pills that I'd managed to convince my parents to buy. I'd often skip breakfast, but that was okay because I'd taken all my vitamins. They'd get stuck in my throat and cause me to keel over in pain, but the important thing was that I had taken my vitamins!

Well, years later (and never mind how many), I have come full circle, back to what I now know is the basis of good health — food!

Nutritional science, through research and study, has taken the food puzzle apart; isolated, labeled, and analyzed each component; extracted the facts; and put it all back together again to give us the sage old advice: fruits and vegetables should be a daily part of our diets because they are so good for us!

This act of breaking foods down to their smallest components (at least as small as science will allow at this time) has taught us many things. That whole foods are nutritious — full of enzymes, vitamins, minerals, and even nutrients we aren't yet able to identify. That eating these foods can protect us from common, modern-day diseases. And that some foods contain more medicinal compounds than others.

From an herbalist's viewpoint, plant foods taken in whole form is the ideal way in which to consume them. The body understands innately how to digest, assimilate, and utilize plant properties. Nature is encoded with its own set of laws, and the human body is not exempt. When we eat *real* food we gain *real* health.

We also understand that plant chemicals work together synergistically. It is the synergy of several or all of the components in the food that is thought to help facilitate the body's own healing, repair, and restoration. Whole foods and plants may also comprise many other necessary and as yet undiscovered compounds.

The isolation and concentration of certain medicinal components may have its place in medicine, but without the benefit of the other phyto-nutrients, the body is forced to work much harder at breaking down the elements. This causes a lot of stress on the system, creating a flood of free radicals (unstable molecules known to accelerate aging) and ultimately causing harm.

Which brings me to maca. Maca is a superfood that is one of those rare finds. Worldwide, maca is gaining a well-deserved reputation that has caught the attention of anthropologists, scientists, botanists, and health professionals because of its vast array of medicinal benefits.

This amazing turnip-like tuber from Peru is chock-full of nutrients and boasts many remarkable healing properties. A hearty cruciferous root vegetable, it has been touted as an aphrodisiac, adaptogen, endocrine balancer, energy enhancer, steroidal, fertility aid, and much more!

As you read through this book you'll come to understand why this wholesome vegetable has become one of my favorite superfoods. It reaffirms our instinct that feeding the body well allows us to live well. Good health is the basis for physical, emotional, mental, and spiritual well-being. As the saying goes, "Fit body, fit mind."

Carmen Mattes

1 THE HISTORY OF MACA

In Peru, knowledge of maca has been passed down from generation to generation. By word of mouth alone, it was said that the root of this plant could revive a weary libido, increase energy, stimulate fertility, improve memory, and relieve depression. Native Peruvians have used this plant to treat tuberculosis and other lung disorders, stomach cancer, convalescence, and hormonal irregularities.

Maca belongs to the mustard family and is the only known cruciferous crop of the Americas. Its history as a very important staple food goes back some 5,800 years.

Archaeological sites show evidence of primitive cultivars dating back as far as 1600 BC. Between 1200 and 100 BC, maca was widely grown and

> *After the Incan conquest of the Andean tribes in 1438, maca became such a highly valued commodity that eventually it was reserved for the exclusive use of royalty and warriors.*

harvested by the Pumpush warriors, who are believed to have domesticated this plant after inhabiting the riverbanks of Lake Chinchaycocha in Junin, Peru. The cultivation of this plant spread to many cultural groups throughout the Andean region. The Yaro Indians — a group known for its outstanding farming abilities — cultivated massive fields of maca, as they held such high regard for the root's rejuvenating qualities.

Food Fit for Kings and Queens

After the Incan conquest of the Andean tribes in 1438, maca became such a highly valued commodity that eventually it was reserved for the exclusive use of royalty and warriors. The warriors were permitted to consume maca only before and during battle. These regulations were put into place to ensure that the women would be safe from the strong aphrodisiac effects that the maca had on the men.

After landing in South America in 1532 and ultimately conquering the Incas, the Spaniards, too, discovered the virtues of this powerful plant, and soon thereafter began exporting it to Spain. In Spain, as in South America, maca was given the royal seal of approval.

In fact, the Spaniards were so impressed with maca that they demanded payment in maca rather than in gold. Historical records also show that over nine tonnes of maca from one Andean region was demanded as payment; and in 1549, the conquistadors sent seven to nine tonnes of maca back to Spain as tribute to the Spanish colonial government. Now that's a lot of cargo to ship across the ocean today — never mind during the 1500s!

High Lands; Low Oxygen

What was it about maca that impressed the Spaniards so much?

Considering that the warring Spaniards had such a general distaste for Incan culture that they tried to obliterate customs, traditions, and anything closely resembling this group, it is intriguing that these conquistadors would fathom the notion of consuming a local food.

Soon after the Spanish conquest, the Spaniards found that their livestock became ill and were unable to reproduce. And not only were the livestock failing to thrive in this new land, so too were the conquistadors. These new inhabitants were being driven out of the highlands, not by their cultural rivals but by their new environmental conditions. Their bodies were unable to adjust to the high altitudes and very low levels of oxygen, which are known to significantly reduce fertility levels, cause great stress to the body, and contribute to poor health.

The natives freely shared their knowledge of maca, which was soon fed to both the livestock and the Spaniards. So successful were its fertility and energy enhancing properties that these successes were recorded extensively in Spanish chronicles.

Close to Extinction

Gradually, knowledge of this plant faded and was almost lost except in very remote areas; only 70 acres of maca could be found in all of Peru, compared with approximately 2,500 hectares of maca that grows in Peru today.

During the 1960s, botanical scientists rejuvenated an interest in maca through their nutritional research at the National University Mayor de San Marcos in Lima. They found that maca contained an astounding array of vitamins and minerals.

Meyenii or Peruvianum?

In 1843, a German botanist named Gerhard Walpers first wrote of maca. He named the plant *Lepidium meyenii Walpers.*

More than a century later, a young biology student named Gloria Chacón first heard of maca from a group of local natives who reported that it had powerful energizing and fertility enhancing properties. Chacón, who attended the National University Mayor de San Marcos in the early 1960s, began studying maca extensively; her dedication to unraveling the mysteries of this almost forgotten natural wonder renewed interest in the plant.

The research conducted by Dr. Chacón resulted in a groundbreaking discovery: previously unknown alkaloids isolated from the maca root were indicated in the increased levels of fertility in the ovaries and testes of rats. Through her field studies in the high Andean region, Dr. Chacón learned that the native peoples not only consumed maca as one of their most important staple foods, but fed the plant to their livestock as well. Her studies confirmed that the consumption of maca increased the animals' libido and promoted healthier, more fertile livestock.

Eventually receiving her PhD and continuing with her research on maca, Dr. Chacón de Popovici (her newly acquired married name) soon became known as the world's leading expert on maca. In honor of her tireless research, the Museum of Natural History in Lima officially named the maca species she had been investigating *Lepidium peruvianum Chacón,* and it was given Registration Number USM:89129 on September 17, 1993. This species is only slightly different from *Lepidium meyenii Walpers.* Botanically and medicinally, the plants are so similar that they are generally considered one and the same.

> *The research conducted by Dr. Chacón resulted in a groundbreaking discovery: previously unknown alkaloids isolated from the maca root were indicated in the increased levels of fertility in the ovaries and testes of rats*

Although both plants are sold on the open market and their names are used interchangeably, many Peruvians continue to use the name *Lepidium meyenii Walpers,* as this is the name they are most familiar with.

Botanical Description

Family:	Brassicaceae
Genus:	Lepidium
Species:	Meyenii, Peruvianum, Peruvianum Chacón
Common names:	Maca, Maka, Maca-Maca, Peruvian Ginseng Maino, Ayak Chichira, pepperweed, ayuk willku
Part used:	Root and leaves
Ethnobotanical Uses:	Anemia, Aphrodisiac, Energy and Endurance, Fertility, Immunity, Impotence, Memory, Hormonal balancer, Stress, Tonifier, Tuberculosis
Properties / Actions:	Antifatigue, Aphrodisiac, Nutritive, Tonic, Steroidal, Immunostimulant
Contraindications:	None
Drug Interactions:	None

Survival of the Fittest

High in the Andes and tucked under a glacial icecap lies the land of this humble root crop. Where no other crop can survive, maca thrives.

The climate of the Peruvian highlands is exceptionally harsh and is subject to extreme weather conditions. The weather conditions in a typical day could range from bone chillingly fierce winds to scorching heat to heavy frosts. The temperature fluctuations from day to night can range as widely as plus 18 to minus 10 degrees Celsius.

Gale winds gust so forcefully that they can evaporate more moisture than the intense sun and blow away more soil than is washed away by the heavy rains. All these weather patterns can occur in a 24-hour period.

Maca seems to flourish best in areas where frost is a common occurrence — the tundra, barren steppes, summits, and high plateaus of the Peruvian Puna and Suni regions. The plant grows at altitudes as high as 14,000 feet above sea level in poor rocky soil that is regarded as some of the most barren and inhospitable farmland in the world! The resilience of the maca plant is, in part, the reason it is so high in medicinal properties. In the herbalist paradigm of thought, herbs that are able to withstand inhospitable elements, diseases, fungi, and parasites bestow this quality of strength and hardiness upon all who consume it.

Maca is a self-fertilizing annual with a two-stage life cycle — a vegetative stage and a reproductive stage. It is a small, flat, low-growing plant with scalloped leaves that produce small white flowers similar to its relative, the mustard family.

It is grown from seed, and is usually planted in the rainy season — September to November. The roots are harvested anywhere from six to nine months after sowing. A typical yield is three tonnes per hectare; but with improved farming techniques, crop sizes are increasing to a hefty 20 tonnes per hectare.

Most maca crops are grown without the use of pesticides or chemical fertilizers. Traditional farming methods use natural fertilizers, such as the manure from local birds. The farmers rotate crops regularly to ensure that the nutrients in the roots will maintain their high quality. However, today, some crops are planted in close proximity to potatoes. These potato crops are grown with large amounts of chemical fertilizers and pesticides. When shopping for your supply, look for labels that specify both non-irradiated and certified organic maca.

Traditional Methods of Consuming Maca

Once plucked from the ground, the plants' leaves and roots are removed, then washed and left in the sun to dry for four to six days. The leaves and roots can then be eaten or stored in a cool, dry place for future use. The dried root can be stored for up to seven years.

The root, or hypocotyl, resembles a small turnip or radish and can be any one of several colors — cream, creamy-purple, purple, or black. The maca hypocotyl is high in protein, starches, sugars, and minerals; and it has a tangy flavor with a lovely butterscotch-like aroma.

Traditionally, native Peruvians eat the root either fresh or dried. Fresh roots are considered a delicacy and are often roasted and consumed like a potato. The dried roots are hydrated by soaking them overnight in water and then parboiling them in milk or water. The boiled roots can then be added to porridge, or liquefied and mixed with juice, jam, pudding, or rum to make a drink called "coctel de maca."

Although they do not contain any medicinal value, the leaves of the maca plant are also utilized. Whether steamed or raw, they are added to salads, and are also used to fatten up the domesticates.

2 NUTRITIONAL AND MEDICINAL PROFILE

Maca is a Superfood

Our SAD (Standard American Diet) eating habits are, truly, contributing factors to so many of the sicknesses we are plagued with on our planet. The way we eat is so far removed from the way our ancestors ate — as Mother Nature intended us to eat — that this subject alone is worthy of much discourse in a separate volume. The stresses of today's high-tech, fast-paced world make consumption of nutritionally dense foods a necessity.

> *Minerals are vital in building and maintaining bone density; and maca contains the minerals that not only prevent, but help to reverse, osteoporosis.*

With its impressive array of nutrients, maca is a good example of a nutritionally dense and therefore valuable source of nutrition. The dried maca root contains roughly 59% carbohydrates, 10% protein, 9% fiber, and 2% lipids. Maca's high mineral content makes it especially appealing, as our typical North American diet is deficient in these essential nutrients. Without adequate mineral intake, the body's uptake of certain vitamins is impeded.

Potassium is one such nutrient. Chemical analysis of maca shows that, proportionately, potassium is the plant's most abundant macronutrient. A primary role of potassium is to work in combination with sodium to balance the fluid levels in the body, as well as the pH levels of these fluids. Potassium also:

- Regulates the heartbeat.
- Aids in the transport of oxygen and other nutrients to the brain.
- Helps to prevent high blood pressure.
- Regulates blood sugar.
- Calms nerves.
- Aids the body in times of stress.

Minerals are vital in building and maintaining bone density; and maca contains the minerals that not only prevent, but help to reverse, osteoporosis.

During stressful situations, the body demands higher amounts of potassium. Maca contains abundant amounts of potassium, calcium, magnesium, silica, copper, iron, zinc, manganese, sodium, and iodine. It also contains vitamins A, B1, B2, B6, C, and E, as well as sterols, tannins, alkaloids, and saponins.

Maca is extremely easy to digest and assimilate. This attribute makes it a superb food for people with faulty digestion, celiac disease, or other intestinal disorders. And because maca is high in fiber, it helps to regulate the bowels and prevent constipation. High fiber is also an important contributor to a healthy heart and cancer prevention.

What Sets Maca Apart?

Although maca's fine assortment of nutrients is striking, it is not specific to maca. What makes maca so unusual is its unique combination of components.

Major Active Constituents of Maca

Alkaloids

Plant-derived alkaloids are compounds that are known for their potent pharmacological activities. Approximately 25% of modern pharmaceutical drugs have been manufactured synthetically using active chemicals from specific plants. Alkaloid chemicals have an established reputation as a group that often excels in the arena of healing complicated ailments. Alkaloids commonly used in pharmaceuticals include digitalis (*Digitalis purpurea*), morphine, and codeine (*Papaver somniferum*), and aspirin (*Salix alba*).

In 1961, Dr. Gloria Chacón de Popovici published research that scientifically demonstrated increased fertility in numerous animal species after being fed maca. She was the first to identify the alkaloids present in maca; and proved that these alkaloids were responsible for the positive results observed in the fertility studies.

The alkaloids identified in the maca tuber include: macaina 1, macaina 2, macaina 3, and macaina 4 (Chacón, 1962); macamides; and macaenes (Zheng, 2000).

In further studies, Dr. Chacón found that, compared with the animals in control groups, rats given either maca root powder or alkaloids isolated from the maca root showed multiple egg follicle maturation in females and significantly increased sperm production and motility rates in males. The effects were measurable within 72 hours of dosing the animals.

Dr. Chacón suggests that the alkaloids in maca act on the hypothalamus / pituitary axis and the adrenal glands. She believes maca has a balancing effect upon the hypothalamus, the master controller of the body, which in turn balances the other endocrine glands, including the pituitary, adrenals, ovaries, testes, thyroid, and pancreas.

Glucosinolates

Glucosinolates (glucosides that contain sulfur) are powerful anti-cancer plant compounds that give cruciferous vegetables their reputation as cancer fighters. They are the compounds that protect the plants from fungi, parasites, and infections. Glucosinolates are responsible for the bitter taste and sometimes strong aroma found in cruciferous vegetables. (The word *cruciferous* comes from the Latin word for *cross,* as the flowers are cross shaped and the plants grow crosswise from the stalk).

Over 100 naturally occurring glucosinolates are found in the diets of many cultures and millions of people worldwide. These compounds tend to be found in cruciferous vegetables such as broccoli, cauliflower, cabbage, watercress, horseradish, turnip, and brussels sprouts.

During digestion, glucosinolates are converted through an enzymatic process into another type of compound called isothiocyanates. Isothiocyanates are potent antioxidants — they are anti-mutagenic and anti-carcinogenic compounds that have proven to be very effective in combating and preventing many different types of cancer. Isothiocyanates have three main functions in the body:

- To prevent carcinogens from becoming activated.
- To neutralize any carcinogens that may have escaped the first line of defense.
- To rapidly eliminate toxic debris from the body.

Methoxybenzyl isothiocyanate is one example of an isothiocyanate found in maca. This compound, however, is not known so much for its anti-cancer properties as it is for its aphrodisiac properties. Scientists believe that methoxybenzyl isothiocyanate is the major compound responsible for maca's aphrodisiac properties.

Indole-3-Carbinol

Yet another extraordinary compound found in maca and other cruciferous vegetables is indole-3-carbinol (I3C), a potent anti-cancer substance. Its use is especially beneficial in hormone-related cancers such as breast cancer and prostate cancer.

In 1991, studies conducted at New York's Institute of Hormone Research demonstrated that cancer rates as well as cancerous tumors significantly decreased in mice and rats fed I3C. A study was then conducted on 25 women, each of whom took I3C for two months. Results showed a decrease in strong estrogen (estradiol — the "estrogen grow signals" that promote cancerous cell growth in the female reproductive organs) and an increase in weak estrogen (estriol). Estriol is a safer form of estrogen that does not encourage cell growth but helps keep the body's estrogen levels at a more balanced state.

> *Yet another extraordinary compound found in maca and other cruciferous vegetables is indole-3-carbinol (I3C), a potent anti-cancer substance*

Research has confirmed that I3C blocks estradiol (the estrogen grow signals) and increases the body's estriol levels. In a study conducted by researchers at Rockefeller University, I3C was found to stop the growth of human cancer cells and to promote apoptosis — the self-destruction of old, abnormal, or infected cells (Telang, Katdare, Bradlow, & Osborne, 1997). I3C also reduces free radical damage, thereby keeping cellular destruction to a minimum.

I3C can now be purchased in supplement form. And while isolating medicinal compounds from foods can have its advantages, it is easier and safer for the body to digest, assimilate, and accept all or any of these compounds when we ingest these foods in as natural a state as possible. Our bodies are meant to assimilate nutrients; and as Hippocrates once said, "Let food be your medicine ... let medicine be your food."

Sterols

Sterols are a large subgroup of steroid-like compounds found in plants and animals. Recently they have generated great scientific interest as they are showing promise in alleviating chronic conditions such as rheumatoid arthritis, diabetes, allergies, cardiovascular disease, and even cancer.

As far back as the 1950s, plant sterols have been known to reduce "bad" cholesterol levels (LDL) by binding to these molecules in the small intestines and attaching to them as they are eliminated by the bowels.

Since then, we have learned that, in addition to lowering cholesterol, the addition of sterols to our diets provides so many more benefits. Plant sterols are now used successfully to treat Benign Prostatic Hypertrophy (BPH), an inflammation of the prostate gland.

One further tremendous advantage for body builders and athletes is that sterols promote lean muscle mass and aid in the burning of fat. They are extremely safe in food form and sure beat the dangers associated with steroid use!

Maca contains several sterols: beta-sitosterol, brassicasterol, erogosterol, stigmasterol, ergostadienol, and campesterol. These sterols aid in lowering cholesterol levels — just one more advantage of consuming maca, a plant that is worthy of study and an excellent substance to add to one's diet.

Saponins

Saponins are yet another beneficial substance present in maca. They are found in many other vegetables, and are currently generating great enthusiasm amongst researchers.

Studies conducted at the University of Toronto's Department of Nutritional Science suggest that the consumption of dietary sources of saponins can reduce the risk of cancer. In fact, saponins are able to inhibit and even kill cancer cells — without destroying healthy cells — by binding to cholesterol molecules. Since cancer cell membranes house more cholesterol-producing compounds than a normal healthy cell, the saponins' process of binding to and excreting cancer cells helps rid the system not only of cancer cells but also of bodily waste.

Dr. A. V. Rao, a Department of Nutritional Sciences professor at the University of Toronto, has been undertaking research to prove that saponins can prevent colon cancer (Lipkin, 1995). When fats are consumed, bile is produced and sent to the small intestine, where it helps to break down and assimilate the fat. But fat in excess produces secondary bile acids, which offer a home to bad bacteria. These bacteria then ferment the bile acids in the colon and produce dangerous carcinogens, which can cause lesions to form on the colon wall. Because saponins naturally bind to cholesterol, and because bile contains cholesterol, saponins are able to bind with these secondary bile acids to flush them out of the body.

Now that we know how saponins work on cholesterol, fat, and bile, we can logically reason that saponins reduce cholesterol levels by clearing excess fat and bile from the colon.

Saponins protect plants from viral, bacterial, and fungal disease. They are, essentially, the active immune system of plant life, consistently demonstrating strong immunological activity with natural antibiotic qualities. Researchers are now looking at ways in which humans might be protected by employing saponins into allopathic medical treatments.

Nutritional Profile of Maca

TABLE 1.   Composition of Maca

Components	%
Water	10.4
Proteins	10.2
Lipids	2.2
Hydrolyzable carbohydrates	59.0
Whole fiber	8.5
Ash	4.9

Sources: Dini, Migliuolo, Rastrelli, Saturnino, & Schettino, 1994. Garró, 1999.

TABLE 2.   Vitamins

Vitamins	mg
B1 Thiamine	0.20
B2 Riboflavin	0.35
C	10.00
E	87.00

Sources: Chacón, 1997.
Garró, 1999.

TABLE 3.   Amino Acids

Amino acids	mg concentration / g protein
Aspartic acid	91.7
Glutanic acid	156.5
Serine	50.4
Histidine	21.9
Glycine	68.3
Threonine	33.1
Cystine	n/d
Alanie	63.1
Arginine	99.4
Tyrosine	30.6
Phenylalanine	55.3
Valine	79.3
Methionine	28.0
Isoleucine	47.4
Leucine	91.0
Lysine	54.3
Tryptophan	n/d
H.O. Proline	26.0

Proline	0.5
Sarcosine	0.7

Source: Dini et al., 1994.

TABLE 4.   Sterols (as steryl acetate derivatives)

Sterol	% of Sterol mixture	Retention time (min)
Brassicasteryl acetate	9.1	22.4
Ergosteryl acetate	13.6	23.8
Campesteryl acetate	27.3	25.0
Ergostadientyl acetate	4.5	27.5
Sitosteryl acetate	45.5	19.5

Source: Dini et al., 1994.

TABLE 5.   Fatty Acids (as methyl ester derivatives)

Fatty acids	% of methyl ester mixture
Dodecanoic (lauric)	0.8
7-tridecenoic	0.3
Tridecanoic	0.1
Tetradecanoic (myristic)	1.4
7-pentadecenoic	0.5
Pentadecanoic	1.1
9-esadecenoic (palmitolete)	2.7
Esadecanoic (palmitic)	23.8
9-heptadecenoic	1.5
Heptadecanoic	1.8
9,12 octadecadienoic (linoliec)	12.6
9-octadecenoic (oleic)	11.1
Octadecanoic (stearic)	6.7

11- nonadecanoic	1.3
Nonadecanoic	0.4
15-eicosenoic	2.3
Eicosanoic (archidie)	1.6
Docosanoic (behenic)	2.0
15 tetracosenoic (nervonic)	0.4
Tetracosanic (lignoceric)	0.4
Fatty acid saturated (%)	40.1
Unsaturated (%)	52.7
Saturated/unsaturated ratio	0.76

Source: Dini et al., 1994.

TABLE 6.   Minerals

Minerals	mg/100g
Fe (Iron)	16.6
Mn (Manganese)	0.8
Cu (Copper)	5.9
Zn (Zinc)	3.8
Na (Sodium)	18.7
K (Potassium)	2,050.0
Ca (Calcium)	150.0

Source: Dini et al., 1994.

3 MACA AND THE ENDOCRINE SYSTEM

The endocrine system is an extremely complex and delicate system of hormonal interchange throughout the body. The endocrine system requires each and every component within it to function optimally. Without this efficiency the whole system is taxed and the repercussions are far reaching

The endocrine system is the central control station that powers our hormones and is largely responsible for our physical, emotional, and mental health. To fully understand how hormones interact in our bodies, we first must understand just how complex our hormonal system is.

Hormones and Communication

Hormones are biochemical messengers that circulate throughout the body, acting as the communication network for the whole organism. Any interference in this communication system triggers a chain reaction that impacts the entire body. This communication breakdown, if left untended, leaves the body vulnerable to accelerated aging. The good news is that we are in complete control of many of the hormones that are important to a youthful and healthy body.

The endocrine system, also known as the glandular system, comprises the hypothalamus, pituitary, pineal, thyroid, parathyroid, pancreas, adrenals, testes, and ovaries, which work continuously to maintain homeostasis — the body's state of physiological and psychological balance. When stimulated by internal and external environmental changes, these glands either release or inhibit the release of various hormones. These glands also produce the hormones that are integral to such complex processes as puberty, menses, menopause, and reproduction; they are also responsible for many characteristics of our physical development, such as height, weight, growth, and maturation.

Unfortunately, the endocrine system is extremely vulnerable and is often one of the first to react to stressors; as a result, it is usually one of the first to become imbalanced. Today we are, collectively, witnessing the results of our malfunctioning endocrine system. And with the recent widespread success and popularity of Viagra™ and Hormone Replacement Therapy (HRT), it is apparent that this fragile system of ours is suffering like never before.

Modern-Day Stressors Deplete our Health

Because our modern-day lifestyles are so hectic and our world is so polluted, our bodies and minds are burdened with enormous pressures. Our food supply has been severely depleted of essential nutrients, our water is impure, and our atmosphere is both oxygen deficient and full of dangerous contaminants. Due to these daily stressors, this unique and highly sophisticated structure is under constant duress. As a result, damage occurs at a cellular level, breaking down the body's internal mechanisms and causing a state of deprivation and potential long-term health issues.

The exciting news is that maca strengthens, nourishes, and balances the endocrine system of both sexes in a gender-appropriate manner. Its action targets the hypothalamus / pituitary axis (HPA), which in turn governs the body's intricate and delicate hormonal system.

Maca has a positive effect on the thyroid, parathyroid, pancreas, and adrenals. Each of these glands becomes balanced and strong as it reaps the benefits of optimum glandular nutrition. With the supplemental aid of maca, symptoms such as impotence, infertility, low libido, PMS, and menopausal hot flashes can all be corrected in a safe, natural, and affordable way.

The Hypothalamus / Pituitary Axis (HPA)

The hypothalamus, also known as the Master Gland, might be considered the most important gland of the endocrine system; it sits deep in the center of the brain behind the eyes, and is directly attached to the small but essential pituitary gland.

The hypothalamus, through stimulation from the central nervous system, regulates body temperature, hormone levels, blood pressure, and blood sugar. In addition, it governs sex drive, hunger, and thirst.

The main purpose of the hypothalamus is to decipher messages from the brain that convey hormone requirements. The hypothalamus then signals the pituitary gland to either release the necessary hormones or to stimulate *other* glands to secrete the necessary hormones (Ley, 2003).

The pituitary gland lies just beneath the hypothalamus and is one of the few components in the brain that has direct contact with the bloodstream. It produces up to 10 different hormones and, once signaled by the hypothalamus, sends out the correct hormone into the bloodstream.

The hypothalamus and the pituitary glands work together within a symbiotic give-and-take relationship. The hypothalamus detects changes in the levels of various hormones in the body and decides whether to increase or decrease their levels by releasing hormones to the pituitary, which, will either promote or inhibit the release of hormones.

Aging and Our Hormonal System

The proper functioning of this intricate communication system is critical. The better this system functions, the slower the body ages; likewise, the less efficiently it operates, the faster the body ages. It has been theorized that the hypothalamus governs the state of health, disease, and aging of the entire organism (Kamen, 1997).

The hormones produced in the hypothalamus and the pituitary axis work in opposition to each other to maintain homeostasis, or balance. It's a little like the balancing act of a set of scales. Each side teeter-totters up and down, striving for a perfect balance as the hormonal levels fluctuate. This dynamic relationship continues every second of every minute, hour, and day, and is in a constant state of flux.

As long as these opposing hormones remain equal in strength, the health of the body will be maintained. Should they become imbalanced, chaos ensues, generating a domino effect throughout the hormonal system, which can become very problematic. .

What makes maca unique is that it acts directly on the hypothalamus / pituitary axis, contributing to the Master Gland's healing, strengthening, and rejuvenating powers.

The Thyroid Gland

The thyroid gland is an integral part of the endocrine system and is the largest gland in the system; it is twice the size in women than it is in men.

> Today, thyroid abnormalities are hitting epidemic proportions in North America, with some endocrinologists suggesting that as many as 27 million people in the United States alone suffer from an overactive or underactive thyroid.

The thyroid has many functions and is one of the most sensitive organs in the body. It is highly adaptive and changes in size, depending on body climate. During a typical menstrual cycle, the thyroid gland changes in size, shape, and activity, then resumes its pre-menstrual size once the cycle is over. Likewise, puberty, menopause, pregnancy, and stress also alter the thyroid gland's shape, size, and activities.

The thyroid produces hormones that govern the physiological system and functions, including metabolism, body temperature, weight, libido, energy levels, and even mood. If the thyroid is not functioning properly, your body will feel rather sluggish on many levels. The biggest complaint is fatigue, followed by fluctuations in weight, reduced mental output, lowered body temperatures, and lack of sexual desire.

Today, thyroid abnormalities are hitting epidemic proportions in North America, with some endocrinologists suggesting that as many as 27 million people in the United States alone suffer from an overactive or underactive thyroid (American Association of Clinical Endocrinologists [AACE], 2005). At least half of these people have not been diagnosed, as the condition is subacute, making it difficult to identify with the current thyroid blood testing procedures. While it is unclear as to why thyroid disorders are on the rise, it is apparent that this gland needs nutritional support, both to repair itself and to protect itself from damage.

According to Dr. Viana Muller, president of Whole World Botanicals, many women have reduced or stopped taking their thyroid medications after supplementing their diets with Maca for three or four months (Moshon, 2003). I do not recommend stopping any medication without medical consultation and testing, but it is clear that natural alternatives such as maca are proving to be safe and effective alternatives.

Although no research has been documented on the effects of maca on the thyroid, we do understand how maca works to properly feed and nourish the endocrine system, thereby giving it the ability to repair and heal itself.

Maca and Depression

Depression in our western culture is growing at an alarming rate, affecting millions of people each year. The World Health Organization (WHO) estimates that, by 2020, depression will be so prevalent, only heart disease will have affected a higher number of people (National Institute of Mental Health [NIMH], 2001). Staggering statistics such as these paint a pretty bleak picture — and that's depressing!

Depression can be tracked in the brain via the neurotransmitters (the brain's messenger system). However, depression is not the result of too few neurotransmitters, as it is a biological disorder stemming from chemical malfunctions in the body. These malfunctions are likely due to miscommunication or slow processing of the body's signals — often a result of poor nutrition.

The World Health Organization (WHO) estimates that, by 2020, depression will be so prevalent, only heart disease will have affected a higher number of people (National Institute of Mental Health [NIMH], 2001)..

Starved for Nutrients

When the body's signals slow down or are no longer able to travel effortlessly, it is often a result of an excess of processed foods, sugar, environmental toxins, and stress. These culprits cause cell membranes to become stiff and rigid, hampering the communication process and blocking vital nutrients an entrance into the cells.

Simply put, the root of depression can be attributed to lack of proper nutrition! Our bodies are starving!

With this realization in mind, two simple steps can help those suffering from depression restore their health and vitality. First, clean up the diet, eat more whole foods, fruits, and vegetables, and begin a regular exercise program.

Second, supplement food intake with nutrients the body may be lacking. You might already have gathered that I consider maca the most effective food for alleviating depression that is hormonally or nutritionally based. A regimen of maca supplements, in combination with hemp and fish oil, is a treatment that will give the cell walls the suppleness they require for efficient nutritional uptake and more effective cellular communication.

4 STRESSING OUT ON STRESS

The Hypothalamus, Pituitary, Adrenals, and Stress

Today, the word "stress" is a familiar term. Most of us have some understanding of the unhealthy effects it can have upon our lives. But what many of us don't know is how stress works in the body, physiologically, and how seriously it can impact our endocrine system.

Stress can directly impact the hypothalamus, pituitary, and adrenal glands. These glands are stimulated by the stress response — also known as the "fight or flight" response.

When triggered by fear, worry, and other stressors, the hypothalamus releases a hormone called corticotrophin (CRH), which triggers the pituitary gland to release another hormone called adrencorticotrophin (ACTH). ACTH travels through the blood stream to find its way to the adrenal glands. The adrenal glands then stimulate production of the stress hormones — cortisol, epinephrine (adrenaline), and norepinephrine.

Stress is negatively implicated in every bodily function, including libido and sexual function, reproduction, menopause, andropause, and menstruation.

As cortisol levels in the blood rise, production of CRH and ACTH fall. This is a typical reaction to stress and is the body's way of taking charge of a dangerous situation. It is now fueled with the hormones to make it more alert, more efficient, and stronger. Uptake of nutrients to the internal organs are restricted, as is digestion and any other function deemed unnecessary to aid in the situation at hand. Yet if the stimulus to continue producing and releasing the hormones is prolonged, then nutrient sources are depleted and the body enters a state of exhaustion.

This response is natural and useful, and once upon a time, it was necessary to preserve life and health. However, this brilliant mechanism was designed to deal with short life-threatening situations, not chronic ones.

Today, we are plagued with worries of both a personal and global nature; we fret about our work, our children, money, global political unrest, and the environment. But none of these concerns threaten our immediate survival. They do, however, trigger the HPA response, resulting in a chronic state of elevated stress hormones.

Defining Stress

Some stress is useful (eustress), as it prepares us for meeting with certain challenges (races, exams, seeing a bear in the woods — and having him see you). Other stress (distress) is harmful.

Physical pain, inflammation, fluctuating blood sugar levels, depression, improper diet, and lack of or too much exercise all stress the body; and the response is exactly the same for each stressor. The body does not discriminate — it simply jumps into action and manufactures the cascade of chemicals necessary to deal with the situation at hand.

Most of us are in a continual state of stress — sometimes acute, but usually chronic. Unfortunately, prolonged stress causes the hypothalamus to trigger more CRH production, and the whole process begins again. With each new wave of CRH, the adrenal glands are forced to produce more and more cortisol and adrenaline, and the roller coaster endlessly cycles.

Adrenal Exhaustion

When the adrenal glands are continually triggered, they quickly weaken and have a much harder time manufacturing cortisol. But cortisol is required not only to trigger but also to shut down production of corticotrophin and adrencorticotrophin (CRH and ACTH). When the hypothalamus and pituitary glands continue sending signals to the adrenals, they have to work harder to do their respective jobs.

The body is already in a state of anxiety due to the overproduction of CRH and ACTH hormones, and now the adrenal function is being compromised too. This vicious cycle creates adrenal exhaustion.

Lack of cortisol due to adrenal exhaustion from prolonged stress results in an overactive immune system. Some conditions linked to depleted cortisol are rheumatoid arthritis, fibromyalgia, depression, hormonal imbalances, and chronic fatigue.

Now, more than ever, we need to equip our bodies with the raw materials necessary to help us cope with our daily stressors. We may not be able to control the world around us, but we can take precautions to ensure that our diet is nutrient rich.

Maca is an excellent superfood. Jam-packed with nutrients that have an enriching effect upon our glandular system, it is most beneficial to our bodies in relation to stress, hormonal health, and general well-being.

The Negative Impact of Excess Cortisol

The amount of cortisol the body requires to function properly stretches a thin line between good health and dangerously ill health. Cortisol is a necessary hormone for regulating blood pressure; reducing inflammation; ensuring proper function-

> *The amount of cortisol the body requires to function properly stretches a thin line between good health and dangerously ill health.*

ing of the immune and cardiovascular systems; and metabolizing fats, carbohydrates, and proteins. In stressful situations, the body needs more energy, which it gets by secreting extra cortisol to help break down and mobilize fats and proteins. And this is where the danger lies.

The key word here is "breakdown." Cortisol is the cellular Break-It-Down hormone and DHEA (a weak androgen) is the Build-It-Up hormone. During times of stress, cortisol levels rise and DHEA levels fall, which results in too much breakdown and not enough buildup. When the gap between these two levels becomes too wide, debilitating effects on our health can occur. And to make matters worse, as we age, our cortisol levels naturally rise and our DHEA levels naturally fall. Getting these two hormones in check before they begin their natural shift is a smart and health-conscious measure that may prevent premature decline.

Cortisol and Immune Function

Cortisol regulates, supresses, and keeps the immune system balanced. This is why chronic stress can have such adverse effects on the immune system.

Additionally, cortisol can have a negative effect on a number of other bodily functions, including digestion, glucose tolerance, fat metabolism (causing weight gain, particularly in the midsection), sleep (interfering with the essential deep sleep known as REM sleep), and memory. Stress is negatively implicated in every bodily function, including libido and sexual function, reproduction, menopause, andropause, and menstruation.

Overproduction of cortisol has been linked to type 2 diabetes, cardiovascular disease, memory loss, depression, sexual dysfunction, premature aging, irritable bowel syndrome, and many other diseases and maladies.

Also associated with the stress response is an excessive release of epinephrine and norepinephrine, which puts us into a state of hyperawareness — the fight-or-flight state. Overproduction of these two hormones causes anxiety, panic attacks, and depression.

> *When it comes to dealing effectively with stress, proper functioning of the adrenal glands is of paramount importance.*

Maca is an Adaptogen

Adaptogens are natural foods, herbs, and other nutritive plants that help increase the body's resistance to disease, strengthen and tone the body's depleted areas, and bring the body back to a state of homeostasis. Adaptogens are non-toxic, non-specific, all-encompassing, and can be safely ingested over long periods of time.

Often referred to as "Peruvian ginseng," maca is a powerful adaptogen. While not a true member of the *Panax ginseng* family, it is an authentic adaptogenic food that exerts a normalizing influence on the body and can help regulate and enhance the endocrine system.

When it comes to dealing effectively with stress, proper functioning of the adrenal glands is of paramount importance. The adrenals are among the most beleaguered glands in the endocrine system; they must endure the brunt of our ever-fluctuating emotional health on a daily and even hourly basis.

It is therefore critical that the adrenals remain vital and healthy, as they are the providers of essential hormones and are heavily relied upon during menopause and times of stress. As an adaptogen, maca effectively tones and strengthens the adrenal glands and, subsequently, the entire body, giving us the ability to effectively resist disease and combat stress.

Rebuilding exhausted adrenal glands takes time, depending on the degree of exhaustion. In most cases, noticeable increases in energy occur within a few weeks.

Other adaptogenic benefits include increased stamina, libido, sexual and immune functions, mental clarity, and a sense of well-being. Many doctors are now recommending maca for elderly patients who want to increase their energy and vigor.

5 MACA FOR SEXUAL ENHANCEMENT AND FERTILITY

Promoting a Healthy Libido

Maca's ability to help restore libido is probably what it is best known for. It is often described as an aphrodisiac for both sexes because of its beneficial effect on estrogen, progesterone, and testosterone. Maca facilitates balance to the hormonal changes of aging and restores a healthy functional status in which both men and women experience a more active libido.

> *How maca works so effectively on the sex drive is intertwined with the hypothalamus' control of sexual appetite. A healthy sex drive depends on the well-being of this important gland.*

To date, numerous studies on both humans and animals have been conducted to investigate the effects of maca on libido. All of these studies have demonstrated that maca significantly increases libido.

Two formal studies have been conducted on human male subjects. These revealed that, while sperm count and motility increased and libido improved, testosterone levels remained the same. What this suggests is that maca does not increase testosterone levels — instead, it re-establishes the body's natural ability to utilize pre-existing hormones more effectively. In other words, maca works to restore the body's default settings and to bring the entire system back to its original, optimum state of health.

Sex (Drive) on the Brain

How maca works so effectively on the sex drive is intertwined with the hypothalamus' control of sexual appetite. A healthy sex drive depends on the well-being of this important gland. The thyroid, ovaries, and testes also play a large role in the libido, so proper functioning of these glands is imperative. Maca works to balance and restore the hypothalamus to optimal condition, which also brings into balance the other glands of the endocrine system.

Although maca has been compared to Viagra™, they function and behave differently from one other in the body. Viagra affects the circulatory system; its action is aggressive and it can behave in an uncontrollable manner. Moreover, the mechanical, non-natural action of Viagra does not address the root of the problem, but instead offers a band-aid solution to a chronic health condition. Viagra can be harmful to one's health, placing the user at risk of developing further physical complications.

While maca may take time to improve a sexual disorder, its therapeutic action works on the core problem and gradually builds up the system to a reasonably functioning sexual state.

Maca is not a stimulant. Unlike stimulants, which can gradually irritate and overstimulate the body systems, maca works to fortify and tone those areas that require strengthening.

Maca Works for Women, Too!

Traditionally, research on aphrodisiacs has focused exclusively on men's sexual potency. But women, too, have long suffered from problems with libido; to date, very few natural products — ones that reverse sexual dysfunction without side effects — have been found. While very little formal data exists regarding the beneficial effects of maca on improving women's libido, all informal reports indicate that maca is very successful in treating sexual dysfunction such as vaginal dryness, painful intercourse, and low libido. Maca, it is reported, enhances natural lubrication of the vaginal area, which softens and tones the vaginal tissue, making intercourse more enjoyable for many women.

It is exciting that maca shows such exceptional promise! Maca is safe, has no side effects, does not interfere with other supplements or drugs, and has been shown to work effectively to combat sexual dysfunction in both men and women.

Teens, Maca, and Libido

A word to all you parents who worry: *don't*. Maca will not send your teenager's libido through the roof. Chances are, your teen's libido is already at an all-time high. My advice is to give maca generously to your teenagers. The addition of a nutrient-packed food to a teenager's often nutrient-deprived diet is a rare and welcome benefit these days. And while maca might not curb your teen's libido, it can certainly help to take the one-track minded edge off — so that your teen can concentrate on his or her schoolwork, household chores, cooperation with siblings. (Well, no — it's not *that* miraculous!)

All joking aside, maca is both an adaptogen and an endocrine balancer, which provides a stabilizing effect on otherwise slightly out-of-control energy levels. Maca cannot turn anyone into a super sex machine. Rather, it works with the natural rhythms of the body to balance the levels of sexual energy.

And as an added benefit, maca can help substantially reduce adolescent acne caused by hormonal imbalances!

Maca and Fertility

Infertility is a growing problem, causing enormous amounts of stress and sadness for many couples trying to start a family. Desperate to conceive, some couples resort to fertility clinics. But costs are very high, numerous invasive medical tests are involved, and the outcome is sometimes multiple births. More often, however, the result is no fertilization at all.

Today, estrogen dominance is a growing concern for both men and women. Industrial byproducts, plastics, synthetic estrogens, and hormonal additives that we find in our food chain are all factors that contribute to our rising estrogen counts. Estrogen dominance can reduce sperm production in men and can negatively affect ovulation in women.

Maca can decrease estrogen, increase progesterone, and free up bound testosterone, which increases libido and improves fertility (Wong, n. d.). In Peru, couples wishing to conceive were once counseled to ingest maca with every meal — to ensure their fertility and bless them with the gift of impregnation.

> *Infertility is a growing problem, causing enormous amounts of stress and sadness for many couples trying to start a family.*

Cultures around the world have gained incredible insights into the powers of plants merely by observing the animals that eat them. These cultures have learned how to identify poisonous plants, edible plants, and plants that have medicinal qualities with healing and life-enhancing capabilities.

Hundreds of years ago, native inhabitants of the land that is now Peru learned not only that maca increases libido, but that a connection exists between maca and fertility. Recent studies have confirmed maca's efficacy as a fertility aid (Lama et al, 1994, Valdivia, 1999). In Peru today, maca is still consumed as it was in the past — as both a food and a medicine for people and animals alike.

Maca and the Birth Control Pill

I am often asked whether maca will interfere with the birth control pill. The answer is no, maca will not interfere in any way.

Maca is a food, not a drug. It is not powerful enough to override the activity of the birth control pill, which is a drug. Thus, consuming maca while taking the Pill will not increase the chances of pregnancy; and by the same token, consuming one substance will not cancel the effects of the other.

Pregnancy and Breastfeeding

Because maca is a food, it is very safe to consume throughout pregnancy. In animal studies, females that were fed maca throughout their pregnancy typically had stronger, healthier, and larger offspring than the groups that were not fed this food (Alvarez, 1993).

Maca is an excellent food for nourishing both mom and baby during pregnancy, and can also be continued successfully during the breastfeeding years.

Personal Note

I took maca before my youngest child was conceived, throughout my pregnancy, and during the breastfeeding stage. When my "maca baby" began eating solids, I added a little powder to his food. Almost four years later, I continue to add maca to his oatmeal in the mornings. I am delighted that his first years have had a very solid nutritional base, which is so important for brain and body development.

And I'm sure the first word he uttered was "maca!"

6 WOMEN'S HORMONAL HEALTH

Menopause Syndrome is a Modern-Day Affliction

By now, most of us have heard something about menopause. Unfortunately, this is because it has become an increasingly difficult transition for many women, wrought with a myriad of physical and emotional symptoms.

But even as recently as 100 years ago, very little reference was made to menopause, people seldom talked about it, and women did not wait in line at doctors' offices in need of support, education, and relief.

In previous decades, public commentary about menopause was virtually nonexistent — not because it was a taboo subject, but because the symptoms simply did not exist. Both menopause syndrome (the negative symptoms of menopause) and PMS are modern-day afflictions that are a direct result of our modern-day lifestyle. In some parts of the world — mostly the rural and so-called "backward" third-world areas — these hormonal difficulties still do not exist. These cultural differences have spawned in-depth debates and discussions by medical bodies worldwide.

We now know that nutritional deficiencies and diets high in sugar, refined foods, hydrogenated fats, caffeine, and alcohol play a pivotal part in contributing to hormonal irregularities. Environmental poisons, poor water, and a lack of minerals in our soil also deplete our reserves and make us more susceptible to imbalances in our reproductive and hormonal systems.

> *Negative menopausal symptoms and the complexities that come with them (what I call menopause syndrome) are inherently related to imbalances in the endocrine system that can be corrected.*

Menopause is NOT a Disease!

What the public has come to accept as the norm is simply not normal or healthy. The body is indeed meant to go through these changes, collectively known as menopause, but it is not meant to suffer through these changes. Menopause is not a disease; it is merely another transitional phase in a woman's life when her menstrual cycle ceases. And just as menstruation should not present us with any unusual or extreme problems, nor should menopause.

Negative menopausal symptoms and the complexities that come with them (what I call menopause syndrome) are inherently related to imbalances in the endocrine system that *can* be corrected. Through proper diet, exercise, and strengthening of the adrenal glands, all of these imbalances can be not only prevented, but completely reversed.

Maca supplies the body with the untreated, unprocessed materials that support the endocrine system in its smooth and efficient operation. Its ability to rebuild the adrenal glands offers great relief to women suffering from severe menopausal symptoms.

Symptoms such as hot flashes, mood swings, depression, fatigue, vaginal dryness, and lack of libido can be corrected both safely and inexpensively.

Maca does not Contain Phyto-Estrogens

Unlike other herbs that are commonly used for menopause, such as black cohosh, soy, red clover, and alfalfa, maca does not introduce weak phyto-estrogens into the body. A phyto-estrogen is a plant-derived substance that has a biological effect, similar to that of estrogen, on humans and animals. Some women are extremely sensitive to these plant hormones — particularly those who go through hysterectomies and experience dramatic estrogen fluctuations, as well as those who are predisposed to certain types of breast and ovarian cancers.

Though they often serve a very useful purpose, plants containing phyto-estrogens can be detrimental to some women, by retarding the body's ability to produce its own hormones. Because it does not promote an imbalance of hormone levels, maca is proving to be a safe and effective alternative to other natural remedies. And because maca does not contain weak hormone-like substances, it benefits both men and women.

Looking for a Safe Alternative

Many women are looking for alternatives to HRT (Hormone Replacement Therapy), especially since the National Institute of Health cancelled its study on HRT in July 2002. This study was conducted on over 16,000 women and was scheduled to run for five years. It came to an abrupt halt when researchers began to see that the women on the HRT had developed an increased risk in breast cancer, heart attacks, strokes, and blood clots. These are very serious consequences and undergoing HRT was clearly not the safest choice.

Maca is very safe, alleviates symptoms, prevents and reverses osteoporosis that is indicative of menopause, and works on the root causes of hormone depletion. Faced with the choice of taking a substance that is included on the US government's official list of carcinogenic drugs or a food that has no known toxicity and works just as well or better than its carcinogenic alternative, most women will choose the latter.

With continuing education in basic nutrition and an understanding of so many common, modern diseases and ailments, it's just good sense to take the necessary measures to protect ourselves against the ravages of menopause syndrome.

Maca and Breast Cancer Prevention

Some women who have had breast cancer or who are considered "high risk" for developing breast cancer have asked if it is safe to take maca. With very good reason, these women are afraid to ingest any substance, natural or otherwise, that may increase their estrogen production.

It is important to understand that the female body naturally produces three primary types of estrogen: estradiol, estrone, and estriol. Drugs such as Premarin®, which are used to enhance the production of estradiol, are composed primarily of the estrone taken from horse urine. In the body, this estrone is then converted into estradiol.

Studies going back as far as 20 years have revealed that, taken in excess, estradiol and estrone increase a woman's likelihood of developing breast cancer. Estriol, on the other hand, effectively protects against breast cancer.

An article in the *Journal of American Medical Association* reported that higher levels of estriol are associated with breast cancer remission; and women who did not develop breast cancer had naturally higher levels of estriol as opposed to estradiol and estrone (Lemon, Wotiz, Parsons, & Mozden, 1966).

Not only is estriol preventative, but it is also proving to be therapeutic in its treatment of breast cancer. It has been compared to Tamoxifen, and actually surpasses this drug in its benefits against breast cancer — without the side effects.

The incidence of breast cancer in vegetarian women and in Asian women is strikingly lower than it is, overall, in North American women.

Estriol has the added benefits of correcting vaginal dryness and thinning of the skin, protecting the cervix and labia, reducing urinary tract infections, and even reducing cellulite!

When balanced and healthy, a woman's body produces the proper ratio of all the different estrogens. Of the three primary estrogens (estrone, estradiol, estriol), estriol has the most protective and positive benefits against breast cancer. At the time of this printing, estriol has not been officially included in any allopathic hormone replacement therapies.

Diet is crucial in the prevention of virtually every disease, including breast cancer. The incidence of breast cancer in vegetarian women and in Asian women is strikingly lower than it is, overall, in North American women. In China, less than 10% of protein intake (fewer than 30 grams per day) comes from animal sources; in North America, roughly 30% of protein consumption (more than 120 grams per day) comes from animals.

Now let's compare breast cancer rates. Breast cancer rates are 70 times higher in North America than they are in China (Duarte, 2003). This statistic leads to at least two assumptions: plant-based diets appear to have an effective disease protection factor and diets high in meat consumption appear to have a disease promotion factor.

Maca is beneficial in the prevention of breast cancer for three reasons.

1. Maca is a cruciferous root vegetable. Cruciferous vegetables such as broccoli and cauliflower have been studied extensively and have proven their worth in the fight against cancer — particularly estrogen-dominant cancers.

    • Cruciferous vegetables contain indole-3-carbinol (I3C), which is now marketed, manufactured, processed, packaged, and sold in its pure form.

I3C has been shown to increase the 2/16 ratio. And what is the 2/16 ratio? The (2) and the (16) represent two metabolic pathways in the liver. The first pathway (2) produces a harmless metabolite called 2-hydroxy-estrone (2-OH E1). The second pathway (16) produces a very toxic metabolite called 16 hydroxy-estrone (16 a-OH E1) that is carcinogenic, overstimulates estrogen receptors, and damages chromosomes. In other words, 2-OH E1 has been shown to inhibit cancer growth and 16 a-OH E1 has been shown to promote cancer growth.

- Because a higher concentration of I3C exists in maca than in other cruciferous vegetables, maca has been referred to as a "superfood."

- Glucosinolates — the substances that give cruciferous vegetables their cancer-fighting reputation — provide excellent protection against breast and endometrial cancer, as well as other types of non-hormonal cancers.

2. Maca is nutritionally dense. It is high in EFAs (essential fatty acids), which have been proven effective in the fight against breast cancer. Maca is also high in fiber. Fiber clears excess fat and estrogens out of the colon, which is very beneficial to breast tissue and the lymphatic system.

3. Perhaps the most important factor is maca's ability to nourish the hypothalamus (master gland), which then regulates the entire endocrine system. This is a very delicate and intricate hormonal system, but with the master gland in top form, all of the other glands tend to come into balance, thereby regulating the hypothalamus' own production of hormones in the proper proportions.

> *Glucosinolates — the substances that give cruciferous vegetables their cancer-fighting reputation — provide excellent protection against breast and endometrial cancer, as well as other types of non-hormonal cancers.*

4. Okay, so there are *four* reasons, not three, why maca is so beneficial, but this one's a no-brainer: maca is a food. It acts as a food in the body. It does not contain any phyto-estrogens and it will not add plant hormones to the body. It works with the body's natural wisdom. This is by far the safest way to achieve a hormonally balanced system. It is completely safe for men, women, children, and pets.

7 MEN'S HORMONAL HEALTH

Addressing Male Menopause

Only very recently have we begun to realize that the elaborate design of the male hormonal system is worthy of notice. Though not all health professionals are convinced that male menopause exists, it is generally agreed that men do go through their own unique physical changes during their middle years — starting anywhere from the early forties and later. Debate about this naturally occurring passage in a man's life is currently piquing the interest of researchers.

> *Testosterone is a very important male hormone that defines a man's maleness — essentially, it is the source of his masculinity, his virility, and his energy.*

Also referred to as andropause or viropause, male menopause is a decline in or an inability to utilize testosterone. Testosterone is a very important male hormone that defines a man's maleness — essentially, it is the source of his masculinity, his virility, and his energy. When this hormone has been depleted, it can have devastating results on a man's health, both physically and emotionally.

Testosterone — Worth its Weight in Gold

Testosterone receptors are cells that line various parts of the body, waiting for the testosterone. They are interlaced throughout a man's body from head to toe; and they are particularly abundant in the heart and the brain. These cells fit the compound like a key fits a lock. Given the high concentration of these receptor cells, it therefore follows that this hormone, testosterone, will naturally play an important role in the many operations of the human male body.

With low levels of testosterone, a man will often show symptoms of:

- Depression.
- Reduced libido (low sex drive).
- Fatigue, lack of energy.

- Lack of ambition.
- Impotence (physical inability to achieve erection / ejaculation).
- Weight gain, especially around the midsection.
- Insomnia.
- Heart disease.
- Prostate conditions, such as inflammation, infection, enlargement of the prostate.
- Moodiness, irritability, lack of enthusiasm for life.
- Muscular atrophy.
- Osteoporosis.
- Type 2 (adult onset) diabetes.
- Loss of mental acuity.

With male menopause, any one or more of these symptoms can manifest themselves. The most common symptoms to appear, initially, are depression, insomnia, loss of libido, irritability, and fatigue.

Clearly, this muscle-building steroidal hormone has a powerful impact on health and well-being, both physically and emotionally. These signs of deficiency clearly show that testosterone is as important to a man as progesterone and estrogen are to a woman. Unfortunately, testosterone deficiency is often overlooked as the cause of many diseases of the modern male.

Fortunately, the number of studies conducted on male menopause is not only increasing, but the research is shedding new light on some very serious male health problems.

In the male body, depletion of testosterone was previously thought to be an inevitable part of growing old. This mid-life "crisis" and most of the common diseases and discomforts associated with it have proven to be reversible. The body's hormonal imbalance can now be restored to a state of more youthful vitality.

Andropause: Three Contributing Factors

Three factors that contribute to male menopause are primary hypogonadism, secondary hypogonadism, and excess estrogen.

Primary Hypogonadism

Primary hypogonadism is when the testicles do not produce enough testosterone. Approximately 90% of testosterone is produced in the testicles; but in some men, the Leydig cells — the cells responsible for testosterone production — lose the ability to secrete testosterone, and low levels of blood testosterone result. A blood test can verify if this is the problem.

Secondary Hypogonadism

In secondary hypogonadism, the Leydig cells in the testicles work just fine, but the hypothalamus, an integral component of the hormonal loop, malfunctions. The hypothalamus has lost its ability to accurately register testosterone levels in the blood, so it does not trigger the pituitary gland to signal the testicles to make more testosterone. A blood test can determine if the problem lies within the hypothalamus / pituitary axis.

An excess of estrogen can have disastrous repercussions for a man, leaving him vulnerable to weight gain, depression, a disinterest in sex, and even at risk for heart attack and prostate troubles..

Excess Estrogen

The third and probably most important contributor to male menopause is not a lack of testosterone, but an excess of estrogen. Men also produce and need estrogen as one of the many components that enhance, regulate, and normalize their complicated hormonal system. However, an excess of estrogen can have disastrous repercussions for a man, leaving him vulnerable to weight gain, depression, a disinterest in sex, and even at risk for heart attack and prostate troubles.

Can Maca Help Resolve Testosterone Deficiency?

While maca itself does not increase testosterone levels, it does allow the body to utilize the free testosterone more efficiently. The free testosterone, which accounts for only 2% of the total amount of testosterone in the male body, is the hormonally active form that can bind to cellular hormonal receptor sites. As men age, substances in the blood bind to the free testosterone, thereby rendering it useless.

Maca's normalizing and strengthening effects on the hypothalamus / pituitary axis is highly effective in reducing and sometimes eliminating symptoms of male menopause. The effects are seen in the ratio of testosterone to estrogen, which brings the hormonal profile back to its proper balance.

Modern science is starting to agree with native folklore that maca can turn back the hands of time and restore the hormonal system to that of its younger years. This is excellent news for men who want to continue to feel virile, potent, and maintain a sex drive well into their later years.

Maca and the Prostate

Unfortunately, benign prostatic hyperplasia (BPH), or enlarged prostate, is present in 50% of men in their fifties, 70% of men in their seventies, and continues along in this vein as age increases (Oliff, 2005). Some researchers believe that if all men were to live long enough, they would all eventually develop BPH or prostate cancer.

With figures like this, it is reasonable to suggest not only that taking an active role in the prevention of prostate conditions is wise, but also that the odds can be beaten with a healthy diet, regular exercise, and reduction of stress.

Maca has a protective effect on the prostate gland for several reasons. First, its nourishing and strengthening effect on the hypothalamus is the first line of defense against any diseases related to hormonal imbalances — not only in the prostate. It is believed that BPH is due to an imbalance in the body's ideal ratio of testosterone (androgens) to estrogen.

Second, maca is high in beta-sitosterol. Beta-sitosterol is a plant sterol that has been used in Europe for several years and is slowly becoming recognized in North America as a viable treatment for BPH. If one suffers with mild to severe BPH, it is worthwhile to supplement the diet not only with maca, but also with other plant-based herbs, such as stinging nettle and saw palmetto.

Published studies have replicated the effectiveness of beta-sitosterol in reducing inflammation of the prostate gland, thus minimizing discomfort and symptoms associated with BPH. As reported in the *British Journal of Urology*, 177 patients were administered 130 mg of beta-sitosterol per day for over six months. Their International Prostate Symptom Scores (IPSS), urinary flow, and residual urine in bladder after voiding were all measured. Results, which demonstrated a significant improvement in the IPSS for patients using beta-sitosterol, were comparable to Proscar®, the drug commonly prescribed for BPH (Klippel, Hiltl, & Schipp, 1997).

In an article published in *Prostaglandins, Leukotrienes & Essential Fatty Acids,* researchers found that beta-sitosterol and resveratrol (a potent antioxidant derived from grape skins) inhibited the growth of prostate cancer cells. They reported that, by itself, beta-sitosterol was more potent and more effective in inducing apoptosis (cancer cell death) than either resveratrol alone or beta-sit and resveratrol combined (Awad, Burr, & Fink, 2005).

> *As a man ages, his testosterone levels drop and estrogen often becomes the more dominant hormone. If prostate cancer should occur, estrogen (estradiol) will stimulate rapid growth of the cancer cells.*

As with breast cancer, indole-3-carbinol (I3C) also protects against prostate cancer. I3C is found in cruciferous vegetables such as broccoli, cauliflower, and cabbage — and it is also found in maca. I3C has been, and continues to be, studied for its reputable benefits in the fight against estrogen dominant cancers.

As a man ages, his testosterone levels drop and estrogen often becomes the more dominant hormone. If prostate cancer should occur, estrogen (estradiol) will stimulate rapid growth of the cancer cells. I3C blocks the effects of estrogen, neutralizing its ability to promote cancer growth, which subsequently allows the testosterone to reclaim its territory.

Maca contains a higher concentration of IC3 than other cruciferous vegetables, which is just one more reason why it is referred to as a superfood.

Although the amounts of beta-sitosterol and I3C found in maca are not as high as the nutrients used in cancer studies, research substantiates the belief that a good diet equals good health. (You are what you eat!) Eating foods that contain these components is an excellent way to prevent and combat disease.

Sterols for a Muscular Physique

Maca is a bodybuilder's dream supplement. In a prize fight for the Olympic gold medal of health, natural sterols (the precursors to steroids) win hands down — with all of the benefits and none of the dangerous side effects!

Sterols found in maca are beta-sitosterol, campesterol, ergosterol, brassicast-erols, and ergostadienol. Some bodybuilders and athletes have used steroids to their immediate benefit but long-term detriment. As a natural alternative, maca not only helps foster lean muscle mass and burn fat, it also increases physical stamina and endurance during a physical workout.

8 CHOOSING AND USING MACA

How to Use Maca

Maca is commonly processed in capsule, tablet, powder, and liquid extract forms. The most economical form by which to deliver maca is powder. Gelatinized powder is the best choice of the powdered forms, as it blends very well with liquids and its active ingredients are more concentrated than they are in other processed forms. Maca powder is very versatile; it can be mixed with

> *Maca powder is very versatile; it can be mixed with water or any hot or cold beverage or food.*

water or any hot or cold beverage or food. My preference is to mix maca with grapefruit juice, add it to a fruit smoothie, or stir it into the morning oatmeal.

What is Gelatinized Maca?

Maca is roughly 50% more concentrated after it goes through the gelatinization process. Gelatinization is an extrusion process that was developed by researchers at the University National Agraria La Molina in Lima. This process removes the starch from the crushed root, and it leaves a more concentrated powder that is easy to digest. And the gelatinized powder mixes nicely into liquids. (No lumps!)

Although gelatinization follows strict guidelines when done properly, some vitamin C will be lost in the process. Nevertheless, most nutrients will stay intact, and it is ideal for anyone suffering from digestive problems.

> *All human clinical trials proving maca's effectiveness have used gelatinized maca (see Appendix)*

All human clinical trials proving maca's effectiveness have used gelatinized maca (see Appendix). Although the standard non-gelatinized maca will obtain the same results, the amount of maca required is much higher, rendering it financially inefficient for use in medical studies, which might make it costlier for the average consumer. Because the gelatinized maca is digested more easily, it is preferred amongst those suffering from gastro-intestinal challenges.

How Much Maca Provides Optimum Results?

It is my experience that the best results are obtained with at least 3,000 mg of gelatinized maca per day. My rule of thumb is to take about double the amount (6,000 mg) if the maca is in its regular, non-gelatinized form.

Because every body is different, with different needs and striving for different results, I have summarized my suggested optimum intake of maca according to the different life stages. These are only guidelines; and you can, of course, create a program that you feel most comfortable with.

> *It is my experience that the best results are obtained with at least 3,000 mg of gelatinized maca per day*

Menopause Syndrome: If symptoms are really severe, it is best to start with 6,000 mg per day, divided into two equal doses of 3,000 mg, to be taken with lunch and dinner. Once symptoms begin to subside to a comfortable level, decrease the total daily dosage to 3,000 mg. After two months' of regular use, my recommendation is to begin cycling maca. This means that you take the maca for three weeks straight, followed by one week's abstinence. Repeat this four-week cycle.

PMS: For pre-menstrual syndrome, 3,000 mg per day should be sufficient. After symptoms subside, it is best to cycle the product. I find the easiest way to do this is to stop taking maca during menstruation and then resume supplementation when the menstrual cycle is over — after approximately one week.

Fertility: The general recommendation (not just mine, but historically) is that both the man and the woman take maca while trying to conceive. For many couples, 3,000 mg per day, taken in the morning, will be adequate. However, if the problem of infertility has been going on for more than two years, you may want to double the amount to 6,000 mg per day until conception occurs. And of course, supplementing with maca can be continued long after conception, through the pregnancy, during the breastfeeding years, and beyond, if desired.

Libido: To increase libido and to maintain these results, it is especially important to cycle maca. Begin with a minimum of 3,000 mg per day as a base amount, then increase or decrease according to your comfort level. After enough time has passed to establish your personalized comfort level, take one week off after three weeks of use. Whether your reasons for supplementing have to do with menopause syndrome, PMS, libido, or any other health issue, you will risk losing the benefit of an increased libido if there is no break in your consumption of maca. A general rule for supplementation is to give the body a chance to remember how to maintain its balances (in this case, hormonal balance), independently and without support of any kind, thereby keeping the internal communication system alert and able to function at its peak.

Body Building: For best results, take 3,000 to 10,000 mg of maca, 60 to 90 minutes before a workout. This gives the maca enough time to digest, yet will allow the sterols and their benefits to remain active in your system during your workout. After approximately one month, you should see a noticeable improvement in your muscle tone!

Some General Guidelines: Because maca is a food, it can be taken with or without meals, and at any time of the day or night. Some people prefer to take it in the morning, as it energizes their day; others prefer to take it before bedtime to help them sleep. For convenience, I take it in the morning. As you become familiar with maca and how it acts in your body, you will get a better sense of how it will work best for you!

Shopping for Maca

When shopping for a maca supplement, be sure to look for brands that are organic, that use only the root, and that are pure (without the fillers that are often substituted for the natural components).

Edibly, Ethically, and Environmentally Friendly!

Because Peru is a third-world country, look for companies who employ fair trade practices with local farmers and who support traditional farming and sustainable harvesting, to ensure the long-term sustenance of maca and its environment. In other words, look for reputable companies who guarantee their product — companies that believe in corporate responsibility and accountability.

Personal Note

Since becoming involved with maca use as a way of life, I have conducted my own personal, academic, and professional research into the benefits of this amazing plant. I have made personal connections with ethical growers and distributors of maca in Peru and in Canada. Sequel Naturals is one such ethically accountable company, whose 100% organic maca product, Macasure, I have been supplementing my family's diets with since 2002. Sequel Naturals and many other companies like it distribute health products wherever the internet and postal service connect. You can also check your local Yellow Pages under Health Food for a distributor in your neighborhood.

For more information about what Sequel Naturals has to offer, I invite you to check out their Web site — where you'll also find other literature I've written on herbs and healthy living — at www.sequelnaturals.com.

9 M-M-M-M-MARVELLOUS MACA RECIPES

Maca is very versatile and can be added to any recipe. Generally, you can aim for one-half to one teaspoon of maca per serving. Just remember to subtract the same amount of flour as the amount of maca you add. For example, if you add one tablespoon of maca, take away one tablespoon of flour. After you've cooked with maca a few times, you will be able to conduct your own taste tests to determine how much maca to add to your recipes.

Any Time is Maca Time!

Breakfast Cereals

1 serving	Oatmeal, pablum, or porridge, cooked
½ tsp	Maca powder

Stir the maca into the cereal for a great way to add maca to the diets of very young children.

Year-round Refreshments

1 serving	Applesauce, chocolate pudding, or fresh fruit smoothie
½ tsp	Maca powder

Stir the maca into any refreshment and watch kids of all ages enjoy the year-round treats!

De-stressful Desserts

"Stressed" spelled backwards is "desserts"!

1 (6 oz) bar	chocolate, dark (Use good-quality dark chocolate, which contains antioxidants that milk or light chocolate do not.
½ tsp	Maca powder

Directions

1. Melt the chocolate in a saucepan over low heat.
2. Stir maca into the chocolate and stir until smooth.
3. Pour into a waxed paper-lined pan.
4. Let it cool and set.

You can try to keep this rich, dark dessert all to yourself, but when your kids discover your secret treasure, you'll have to keep a ready supply on hand. (And they'll never know they're eating a healthy treat!)

Smoothies

The Macagizer

1	Banana, ripe
½ cup	Ice, crushed
½ cup	Milk or water (I like coconut or soy milk.)
¼ cup	Flax seeds, freshly ground
1 Tbsp	Ovaltine or cocoa powder
1 Tbsp	Maca powder
2 Tbsp	Hemp, soy, or rice protein powder

Directions

1. Blend the ice, banana, and water or milk until smooth.
2. Gradually add the remaining ingredients.
3. Pour into tall milkshake glasses and enjoy!

Makes two regular servings or one gigantic shake! Drink this in lieu of breakfast for a week and you'll know what it means to feel maca-gized!

Tropical Smoothie

1 cup	Pineapple juice, cold
½ cup	Strawberries
½ cup	Mango, diced
1	Orange, peeled
2 tsp	Maca powder
½ cup	Coconut milk (optional)

Blend ingredients until smooth, then pour into tall milkshake glasses and serve. YUM!

The Brain Pleaser

1 cup	Blueberries
½ cup	Strawberries
½ cup	Raspberries
½ cup	Cream, soya milk, almond milk, coconut milk, or rice milk (your choice)
½ to 1 cup	Fruit juice
2 tsp	Maca powder
1 Tbsp	Flax or hemp oil

Blend ingredients until smooth, then pour into tall milkshake glasses and enjoy

Muffins

Bran-Maca Muffins

¼ cup	Butter
½ cup	Honey
¼ cup	Molasses
2	Eggs
1 cup	Milk (Almond milk and soy milk are my preferences.)
¾ cup	Spelt flour
¼ cup	Maca powder
1 ½ tsp	Baking powder
½ tsp	Baking soda
¾ tsp	Salt
1 ½ cups	Bran
½ cup	Raisins, grated carrots, or grated apple

Directions

1. Preheat oven to 375 to 400 degrees F.
2. Cream shortening and honey together.
3. Add molasses and eggs, and beat well.
4. Add milk, bran, and fruit.
5. Sift dry ingredients into the batter, and blend. Do not overmix.
6. Pour into muffin tins, to three-quarter fullness.
7. Bake for 18 to 20 minutes or until golden brown.
8. Serve warm for a tasty, high-fiber snack.

Makes 12 muffins.

Cran-nana Maca Muffins

This is something the whole family will enjoy!

In a large bowl, combine dry ingredients:

4 cups	Flour
½ cup	Maca powder
2 ¼cups	Brown sugar
3 tsp	Baking powder
3 tsp	Baking soda
1 ½ tsp	Salt
3 tsp	Cinnamon

In a separate bowl, combine wet ingredients:

1 ½ cups	Olive oil
3 cups	Cranberries
3 cups	Banana
1 ½ cups	Chocolate chips
2 ½ cups	Milk

Directions

1. Preheat oven to 325 to 350 degrees F.
2. Add wet ingredients to dry ingredients, and blend until just mixed. Do not overmix.
3. Pour into muffin tins, to three-quarter fullness.
4. Bake for 20 to 30 minutes or until golden brown.

Makes 48 muffins.

APPENDIX: MACA ABSTRACTS

Libido Enhancement and Sexual Performance Studies

Cicero, A. F., Bandieri, E., & Arletti, R. (2001). Lepidium meyenii Walpers improves sexual behavior in male rats independently from its action on spontaneous locomotor activity. *Journal of Ethnopharmacology, 75, (2-3), 225-229.*

> *Lepidium meyenii Walpers (maca) is traditionally employed in the Andean region for its supposed properties to improve energy and fertility. The aim of this study was to evaluate the effect of acute and chronic maca pulverized root oral administration on rat sexual behavior.*
>
> *Sixty male sexually experienced rats (20 group) were daily treated for 15 days with maca 15 mg kg(-1), maca 75 mg kg(-1) or saline 0.5 ml kg(-1). An activity cage test was carried out to evaluate if maca-induced locomotion changes could indirectly improve rat sexual performances. It was concluded that both acute and chronic maca oral administration significantly improve sexual performance parameters in male rats.*

Gonzales, G. F., Cordova, A., Vega, K., Chung, A., Villena, A., & Gonez, C. (2003). Effect of lepidium meyenii (maca), a root with aphrodisiac and fertility-enhancing properties, on serum reproductive hormone levels in adult healthy men. *Journal of Endocrinology, 176 (1), 163-168.*

> *This study was a 12-week double-blind, placebo-controlled, randomized, parallel trial in which active treatment with dif-*

ferent doses of gelatinized maca was compared with a placebo. The study aimed to test the hypothesis that maca has no effect on serum reproductive hormone levels in apparently healthy men when administered in doses used for aphrodisiac and / or fertility-enhancing properties. Men aged between 21 and 56 Years received 1,500 mg or 3,000 mg maca. Serum levels of luteinizing hormone, follicle-stimulating hormone, prolactin, 17-alpha hydroxyproges-terone, testosterone and 17-beta estradiol were measured before and at 2, 4, 8 and 12 weeks of treatment with place-bo or maca.

Data showed that compared with placebo maca had no effect on any of the hormones studied nor did the hormones show any changes over time. Multiple regression analysis showed that serum testosterone levels were not affected by treatment with maca at any of the times studied (P=NS). In conclusion, treatment with maca does not affect serum reproductive hormone levels.

Gonzales, G. F., Cordova, A., Vega, K., Chung, A., Villena, A., Gonez, C., et al. (2002). Effect of lepidium meyenii (maca) on sexual desire and its absent relationship with serum testosterone levels in adult healthy men. *Andrologia, 34 (6),* 367-372.

This study was a 12-week double blind placebo-controlled, randomized, parallel trial in which active treatment with dif-ferent doses of gelatinized maca was compared with place-bo. The study aimed to demonstrate if effect of maca on sub-

jective report of sexual desire was because of effect on mood or serum testosterone levels.

Men aged 21-56 years received maca in one of two doses: 1,500 mg or 3,000 mg or placebo. Self-perception on sexual desire, score for Hamilton test for depression, and Hamilton test for anxiety were measured at 4, 8 and 12 weeks of treatment. An improvement in sexual desire was observed with maca since 8 weeks of treatment. Serum testosterone and oestradiol levels were not different in men treated with maca and in those treated with placebo (P=NS).

Logistic regression analysis showed that maca has an independent effect on sexual desire at 8 and 12 weeks of treatment, and this effect is not because of changes in either Hamilton scores for depression or anxiety or serum testosterone and oestradiol levels. In conclusion, treatment with maca improved sexual desire.

Zheng, B. L., He, K., Kim, C. H., Rogers, L., Shao, R. V., Huang, Z. Y., et al. (2000). Effect of a lipid extract from Lepidium meyenii on sexual behavior in mice and rats. *Urology, 55,* 598-602.

This clinical study evaluates the effect of a purified lipidic extract of Lepidium meyenii (maca) in the sexual behavior of mice and rats. Oral administration of maca extract enhanced the sexual function of the mice and rats, as evidenced by an increase in the number of complete intromissions and the number of sperm-positive females in normal mice, and a decrease in the LPE in male rats with erectile dysfunction. The present study reveals for the first time an aphrodisiac activity of L. meyenii, an Andean mountain herb.

Energy and Stamina Studies

Gayoso, O., Aguilar, J. L., Goyzueta, I., Rojas, P., Marcelo, A., Timoteo, O., et al. (n. d.). *Effect of lepidium meyenii (maca) on physical-energetic performance in humans.* Retrieved October 13, 2002, from www.pubmed.gov

In this prospective double blind placebo controlled study it is demonstrated that exists an improvement in the physical yield of healthy adults supplemented with Lepidium meyenii (maca) on a daily dose, which is significantly superior to the yield of the placebo group. An increase in the distance range in the six-minute walking test (SMW7J in people from maca group (p< 0.05) was demonstrated. No modifications in weight or biochemical nutritional parameters were detected, thus this stamina property is independent of nutritional features of maca. No side effects were reported with ingestion of maca.

Miura, T., Hayashi, M., Naito, Y., & Suzuki, I. (1999). Anti-hypoglycemic effect of maca in fasted and insulin-induced hypoglycemic mice. *Journal of Traditional Medicine, 16,* 93-96.

In this clinical trial, the anti-hypoglycemic effect of Lepidium meyenii was investigated in fasted and insulin-induced

hypoglycemic mice. The results indicated the anti-hypo-glycemic effect of Lepidium meyenii may promote glyconeo-genesis. These findings may be useful for the treatment of energy supply on hypoglycemic conditions.

Rojas, P., Macarlupu, J. L., Capcha, R., Plaza, A., & Aguilar, J. L. (n. d.). *Evaluation of the stamina activity of two extracts from lepidium meyenii (maca) in albino mice.* Retrieved October 13, 2002, from www.pubmed.gov

In this study two standardized extracts of Lepidium meyenii with a known concentration of glucosinolates were evaluated by the stamina effect in mice using the oxygen consumption (the VO2 max) in rest and after activity. The results show a significant increase of energetic performance of mice supplemented with glucosinolate-enriched extracts compared to control group no supplemented. This study increases the amount of evidence about the energetic capability of maca in animal models.

Salas, C. A. (n. d.). *Vigor-inducing effect of maca (Lepidium meyenii Walpers): An Andean hypocotyl, in mice.* Retrieved October 13, 2002, from www.pubmed.gov

In this study a group of mice supplemented with Lepidium meyenii were compared to control group to evaluate the stamina effect. The results show a significant increase of energetic performance in oxygen consumption, and also an increase of resistance on swimming time. These results show the vigor-inducing effect of maca.

Hormonal and Fertility Studies

Alvarez, C. (1993). *Utilízación de diferentes niveles de maca en la fertilidad de cobayos.* Resumen de Tesis de Ingeniero Zootecnista, Universidad Nacional Daniel Alcides Carrion, Cerro de Pasco, Perú:

> *This is a biological study in guinea pigs focusing the utilization of different amounts of supplementation with Lepidium meyenii to evaluate the number and characteristics of offspring. Results show an increase in number of descendent in a direct relationship to amount of supplementation of maca. The quality of offspring is also improved by the supplementation with maca.*

Apumayta, U. P., & Cuba, P. (n. d.). Separation of active principles of hexanic extract of lepidium meyenii Walpers. In *Proceedings of the Congreso de Investigación, Lima, Peru.* Retrieved October 13, 2002, from www.pubmed.gov

> *This abstract was presented in a Peruvian Congress that reported the use of a hexanic extract of maca in post-menopausal women. The serum levels of luteinizing hormone (frequently increased in post-menopausal women) decrease from 117,189 mUl/lmL previous supplementation to 32,03 mUl/lmL after treatment.*

Lama, G., Quíspe, G., Ramos, D., Ferreyra, C., Casas, H., & Apumayta, U. (1994). Study of the estrogenic property of maca in rats. In *Proceedings of the congreso nacional de ciencias farmacéuticas y bioquímicas, Lima, Peru.* Retrieved October 13, 2002, from http://www.indecopi.gob.pe/tribunal/propiedad/InformeMaca.pdf

This is an abstract report presented in the Peruvian Congress of Pharmacy. It is a short report referring to pro-estrogenic effects of the administration of a hexanic extract of Lepidium meyenii. The increased weight of ovaries was the main feature to consider pro-estrogenic effect showed by treated group.

Valdivia, M. (1999). *Protector effect of maca in the testicular function of mice treated with oral imidazol.* Lima: Universidad Nacional Mayor de San Marcos.

This is a biological study on mice focusing on the protective effects of maca on the testicular production of spermatozoids. In this study the production of spermatozoids is damage for an overdose use of imidazolic compound and they observe that the group of mice supplemented with maca had better recovery of spermatozoid production in comparison with control group. This results shows cytoprotective effect on sperm cell line or increase of recovery capacity provided by maca.

Nutritional Studies

Canales, M., Aguilar, J., Prada, A., Marcelo, A., Huaman. C., & Carbajal, L. (2000). Nutritional evaluation of Lepidium meyenii (maca) in albino mice and their descendants. *Archives of Latin American Nutrition, 50 (2),* 126-133.

With the purpose of scientifically evaluating the nutritional property of maca, we carried out a controlled study in two generations of albino Swiss mice (parents and breeding).

The parents were aleatorily assigned to one of three nutritional schedules. The food of each group was prepared based on powder from a commercial balanced food (CBF) of which 30 percent was replaced by raw or cooked maca according to the corresponding group or pure CBF in the control group.

The groups were this way: 1) Raw Maca Group; 2) Cooked Maca Group; and, 3) Control Group. The results showed that the curves of growth were similar and adequate for the three groups. However, the cooked maca group showed the best curve. The CBF group had a better growth than raw maca group. This study demonstrates, in a scientific evaluation, the nutritional capability of maca.

Piacente, S., Carbone, V., Plaza, A., Zampelli, A., & Pizza, C. (2002). Investigation of the tuber constituents of maca (lepidium meyenii Walpers). *Journal of Agricultural Food Chemistry, 50 (20)*, 5621-5625.

Lepidium meyenii, known in South America as maca, has received attention worldwide as a powerful energizer that improves physical and mental conditions and increases fertility. Because of these reports, we investigated the secondary metabolites of the tuber of maca. The methanol extract of the tuber of maca contained, in addition to free sugars and amino acids, the following: uridine, malic acid and its benzoyl derivative, and the glucosinolates, glucotropaeolin and m-methoxyglucotropaeolin.

Because glucosinolates and their derived products have received increasing attention due to their biological activities, the occurrence of glucosinolate degradation products in the hexane extract was also investigated, and benzylisothiocyanate and its m-methoxy derivative were isolated. The two glucosinolates were semiquantified by HPLC, and benzylisothiocyanate was semiquantified by GC/MS. The methanol extract of maca tuber also contained (1R,3S)-1-methyltetrahydro-beta-carboline-3-carboxylic acid, a molecule that is reported to exert many activities on the central nervous system.

Anti-Stress and Toxicity Studies

Capcha, R., Marcelo, A., Rojas, P., Ramos, A., Plaza, A., & Aguilar, J. L. (n. d.). *Acute toxicity — determination of lethal doses for standardized extracts of maca.* Retrieved October 13, 2002, from www.pubmed.gov

In this study the acute toxicity (DL50) of two extracts of maca provided by Química Suiza were evaluated. The extracts were administered by oral via in Swiss mice by a period of 3 days. The results show a DL50 greater of 68 070 mg/Kg, dose in which not death of mice were registered, nor either changes in the behavior, or some alteration in the internal organs. Therefore this study demonstrates the absence of acute toxicity of maca extracts in Swiss mice, dosed orally.

Capcha, R., Marcelo, A., Rojas, P., Ramos, A., Plaza, A., & Aguilar, J. L. (n. d.). *Anti-stress effect of two extracts of maca enriched in glucosinolates.* Retrieved October 13, 2002, from www.pubmed.gov

In this study a group of BaLB/C strain mice (Mus musculus) of 50-60 days of age and 20-30 weigh were used to evaluate the anti-stress activity of an extract of Lepidium meyenii. The animals were dosed with maca extracts enriched with glucosinolates that were inoculated via oral by needle for 100 days. Stress was induced by electrical stimulation, which served to evaluate the development of neurotic features using the modified Lopez scale. Results showed that the extracts from maca enriched with glucosinolates had a significantly better anti-stress activity compared to the control group.

Marcelo, A., Okuhama, N., Mairena, T., Salazar, M., & Aguilar, J. L. (n. d.). *Absence of acute toxicity and cytotoxicity in-vitro of lepidium meyenii.* Retrieved October 13, 2002, from www.pubmed.gov

Acute toxicity was determined in the animal model. Increasing amounts of maca were orally administered to Swiss mice, which were observed for a 3 day-period. From low doses to 800ug/mL of the aqueous extract showed no changes in viability. Both evaluations show very good tolerance of in vitro and ín vívo assays for maca.

Tapia, A., López, C., Marcelo, A., Canales, M., & Aguilar, J. L. (2000). Maca and its anti-stress effect on an animal model in mice. *Acta Andina, 8,* 31-37.

Maca has been traditionally mentioned as an anti-stress natural product. This clinical study evaluates the effect of Lepidium meyenii in the control of stress compared to a control group, in an experimental induce stress in mice. The results show significant less score of stress in supplemented group compared to control. Also the supplemented group had more rapid normalization of stress than control group. This study shows the anti-stress effect of maca in an animal model.

BIBLIOGRAPHY

Alvarez, C. (1993). *Utilízación de diferentes niveles de maca en la fertilidad de cobayos.* Resumen de Tesis de Ingeniero Zootecnista, Universidad Nacional Daniel Alcides Carrion, Cerro de Pasco, Perú:

American Association of Clinical Endocrinologists. (2005). *Thyroid fact sheet.* Retrieved July 17, 2006, from www.aace.com

Apumayta, U. P., & Cuba, P. (n. d.). Separation of active principles of hexanic extract of lepidium meyenii walpers. In *Proceedings of the Congreso de Investigación, Lima, Peru.* Retrieved October 13, 2002, from www.pubmed.gov

Awad, A. B., Burr, A. T., & Fink, C. S. (2005). Effect of reseveratrol and beta-sitosterol in combination or reactive oxygen species and prostaglandin release by PC-3 cells. *Prostaglandins, Leukotrienes & Essential Fatty Acids, 72 (3),* 219-26.

Balick, M. J., & Lee, R. (2002). Maca: from traditional food crop to energy and libido stimulant. *Alternative Therapies in Health and Medicine, 8 (2),* 96-98.

Bouic, P. D., Patrick, J. D., & Lamprecht, J. H. (1999). Plant sterols and sterolins: A review of their immune modulating properties. Alternative Medicine Review, 4 (3), 170-177.

Canales, M., Aguilar, J., Prada, A., Marcelo, A., Huaman. C., & Carbajal, L. (2000). Nutritional evaluation of Lepidium meyenii (maca) in albino mice and their descendants. *Archives of Latin American Nutrition, 50 (2),* 126-133.

Capcha, R., Marcelo, A., Rojas, P., Ramos, A., Plaza, A., & Aguilar, J. L. (n. d.). *Acute toxicity: Determination of lethal doses for standardized extracts of maca.* Retrieved October 13, 2002, from www.pubmed.gov

Capcha, R., Marcelo, A., Rojas, P., Ramos, A., Plaza, A., & Aguilar, J. L. (n. d.). *Anti-stress effect of two extracts of maca enriched in glucosinolates.* Retrieved October 13, 2002, from www.pubmed.gov

Cardenas, R. A., & Quiros, C. M. (1997). Maca lepidium meyenii. In M. Hermann & J. Heller (Eds.), Andean roots and tubers: Ahipa, arracacha, maca, yacon — promoting the conservation and use of underutilized and neglected crops. Rome: International Plant Genetic Resources Institute.

Carruthers, M. (2001). *Testosterone revolution: Rediscover your energy and overcome the symptoms of the male menopause.* New York: Thorsons Publishing Group.

Chevalier, A. (1996). Maca. *Encyclopedia of medicinal plants: A practical reference guide to more than 550 key medicinal plants and their use.* New York: Dorling Kindersley.

Chacón, G. La importancia de Lepidium peruvianum Chacón ("maca") en la ali-
mentacion y salud del ser humano y animal 2,000 años antes y despues
de Cristo y en el siglo XXI. (1997). Lima: Servicios Gráficos "Romero".
Retrieved February 23, 2002, from http://www.ecoandino.com

Cicero, A. F., Bandieri, E., & Arletti, R. (2001). Lepidium meyenii walpers
improves sexual behavior in male rats independently from its action
on spontaneous locomotor activity. *Journal of Ethnopharmacology,
75, (2-3),* 225-229.

Cicero, A. F., Piacente, S., Plaza, A., Sala, E., Arletti, R., & Pizza, C. (2002).
Hexanic maca extract improves rat sexual performance more effectively than methanolic and chloroformic maca extracts. *Andrologia,
34 (3),* 177-179.

Diamond, Jed. (1998). *What is male menopause? Information from the book
male menopause.* Retrieved November 23, 2002, from
http://www.menalive.com/menowhat.htm

Dini, A., Migliuolo, O., Rastrelli, L., Saturnino, P., & Schettino, O. (1994).
Chemical composition of lepidium meyenii. *Food Chemistry, 49,* 347-349.

Duarte, A. (Producer). (2003). *Living longer and loving it: How to prevent, stop,
and reverse the aging process.* St. George, UT: Tree of Light Publishing.

Dyer, D. (2000). *Cellfood: Vital cellular nutrition for the new millennium.*
New York: Feedback Books.

Garró, V. (1999). *Macro y micro elementos de la maca.* Retrieved October 13, 2002, from www.pubmed.gov

Gayoso, O., Aguilar, J. L., Goyzueta, I., Rojas, P., Marcelo, A., Timoteo, O., et al. (n. d.). *Effect of lepidium meyenii (maca) on physical-energetic performance in humans.* Retrieved October 13, 2002, from www.pubmed.gov

Gonzales, G. F. (1989). Functional structure and ultrastructure of seminal vesicles. *Archives of Andrology, 22,* 1-13.

Gonzales, G. F., Cordova, A., Gonzales, C., & Chung, A. (2001). Lepidium meyenii (maca) improved semen parameters in adult men. *Asian Journal of Andrology, 3 (4),* 301-303.

Gonzales, G. F., Cordova, A., Vega, K., Chung, A., Villena, A., & Gonez, C. (2003). Effect of lepidium meyenii (maca), a root with aphrodisiac and fertility-enhancing properties, on serum reproductive hormone levels in adult healthy men. *Journal of Endocrinology, 176 (1),* 163-168.

Gonzales, G. F., Cordova, A., Vega, K., Chung, A., Villena, A., Gonez, C., et al. (2002). Effect of lepidium meyenii (maca) on sexual desire and its absent relationship with serum testosterone levels in adult healthy men. *Andrologia, 34 (6),* 367-372.

Gonzales, G. F., Ruiz, A., Gonzales, C., Villegas, L., & Córdova, A. (2001). Effect of lepidium meyenii (maca) roots on spermatogenesis of male rats. *Asian Journal of Andrology, 3 (3),* 231-233.

Hastings, C. M. (2001). Outline: Environmental studies 101. Retrieved September 15, 2002, from http://www.chsbs.cmich.edu/ charles_hastings / Courses/ENV101_Lec.htm

Johns, T. (1981). The anu and the maca. *Journal of Ethnobiology, 1,* 208-212.

Kamen, B. (1997). *Hormone replacement therapy: Yes or no?* (6th ed.). Novato, CA: Nutrition Encounter.

Keith, V. J., & Gordon, M. (1984). *The how to herb book.* Mountain View, CA: Mayfield Publications.

Kiefer, Dale. (2006, January). I3C & DIM: Natural, dual action protection against deadly cancers. *Life Extension Magazine.* Retrieved February 6, 2006, from http://www.lef.org

Klippel, K. F., Hiltl, D. M., & Schipp, B. A. (1997, September). Multicentric, placebo-controlled double blind clinical trial of beta-sitosterol (phytosterol) for the treatment of benign prostatic hyperplasia. German BPH Phyto Study group. *British Journal of Urology, 80 (3):* 427-32.

Lama, G., Quíspe, G., Ramos, D., Ferreyra, C., Casas, H., & Apumayta, U. (1994). Study of the estrogenic property of maca in rats. In *Proceedings of the congreso nacional de ciencias farmacéuticas y bioquímicas, Lima, Peru.* Retrieved October 13, 2002, from http://www.indecopi.gob.pe/tribunal/propiedad/InformeMaca.pdf

Lemon, H. M., Wotiz, H. H., Parsons, L., & Mozden, P. J. (1966). Reduced estriol excretion in patients with breast cancer prior to endocrine therapy. *JAMA, 196.* 112-120.

Leon, J. (1964). The "maca" (lepidium meyenii): A little known food plant of Peru. *Economic Botany, 18,* 122-127.

Ley, B. M. (2003). *Maca: Adaptogen and hormonal regulator.* Detroit Lakes, MN: B. L. Publications.

Lipkin, R. (1995, December). Vegemania: Scientists tout the health benefits of saponin. *Science News, 148 (24): 382.*

Lipton, B. (2005). *The biology of belief: unleashing the power of consciousness matter and miracles.* Santa Rosa, CA: Mountain of Love / Elite Books.

Male hormone modulation therapy. (n. d.). Retrieved March 3, 2003, from http://www.lef.org/protocols/prtcl-130.shtml

Marcelo, A., Okuhama, N., Mairena, T., Salazar, M., & Aguilar, J. L. (n. d.). *Absence of acute toxicity and cytotoxicity in-vitro of lepidium meyenii.* Retrieved October 13, 2002, from www.pubmed.gov

Miura, T., Hayashi, M., Naito, Y., & Suzuki, I. (1999). Anti-hypo-glycemic effect of maca in fasted and insulin-induced hypoglycemic mice. *Journal of Traditional Medicine, 16,* 93-96.

National Institute of Mental Health (NIMH). (2001, March). *The unwanted co-traveler: Depression's toll on other illnesses.* Forum conducted at The Unwanted Co-traveler: A Day for the Public, Pittsburgh, PA.

National Research Council. (1990). *Lost crops of the Incas: Little known plants of the Andes with promise for worldwide cultivation.* Washington, DC: National Academy Press.

O'Brian, Chris. (2002, March). Sterols: Formidable disease fighter. *Functional Foods and Nutraceuticals.* Retrieved January 15, 2003, from http://www.newhope.com/ffn/ffn_backs /mar_02/sterol.cfm

Oliff, Heather S. (2005). A powerful addition to herbal prostate support. *Life Extension Magazine.* Retrieved February 6, 2006, from http://www.lef.org

Piacente, S., Carbone, V., Plaza, A., Zampelli, A., & Pizza, C. (2002). Investigation of the tuber constituents of maca (lepidium meyenii walpers). *Journal of Agricultural Food Chemistry, 50 (20),* 5621-5625.

Popenoe, H. (1990). *Lost crops of the Incas.* Washington, DC: National Academy Press, 5761.

Rea, J. (1994). Maca: Lepidium meyenii. In J. E. Hernando & J. Leon (Eds.), Neglected crops: 1492 from a different perspective. *Plant Production and Protection* (Series No. 26, 165-179). Rome: F. A. O.

Riedel W. J. (2002). *Depletion of body chemical can cause memory mood changes.* Retrieved July 16, 2005, from http://www.cfah.org/hbns/news/chemical11-18-02.cfm

Rojas, P., Macarlupu, J. L., Capcha, R., Plaza, A., & Aguilar, J. L. (n. d.). *Evaluation of the stamina activity of two extracts from lepidium meyenii (maca) in albino mice.* Retrieved October 13, 2002, from www.pubmed.gov

Shomon, M. (2003). *A look at South American medicinal herbs and hormonal health: An interview with Dr. Viana Muller.* Retrieved July 17, 2006, from www.thryoid.about.com

Salas, C. A. (n. d.). *Vigor-inducing effect of maca (Lepidium meyenii walpers): An Andean hypocotyl, in mice.* Retrieved October 13, 2002, from www.pubmed.gov

Sears, B. (2000). *The age free zone.* New York: Regan Books.

Shippen, E., & Fryer, W. (1998). *The testosterone syndrome: The critical factor for energy, health, & sexuality — reversing the male menopause.* New York: M. Evans and Company, Inc.

Tapia, A., López, C., Marcelo, A., Canales, M., & Aguilar, J. L. (2000). Maca and its anti-stress effect on an animal model in mice. *Acta Andina, 8,* 31-37.

Taylor, L. (1998). Maca. In *Herbal secrets of the rainforest: The healing power of over 50 medicinal plants you should know about.* Austin, TX: Prima Publishing, Inc.

Telang, N. T., Katdare, M., Bradlow, H. L, & Osborne, M. P. (1997). Estradiol metabolism: An endocrine biomarker for modulation of human mammary carcinogenesis. *Environmental Health Perspectives, 105 (3),* 559–564.

Tellez, M.R., Khan, I.A., Kobaisy, M., Schrader, K.K., Dayan, F.E., & Osbrink, W. (2002). Composition of the essential oil of lepidium meyenii (walpers). *Phytochemistry, 61 (2),* 149-155.

Tropical plant database file for maca (lepidium meyenii). (2001). Retrieved September 17, 2002, from http://www.rain-tree.com/maca.htm

Valdivia, M. (1999). *Protector effect of maca in the testicular function of mice treated with oral imidazol.* Lima: Universidad Nacional Mayor de San Marcos.

Walker, M. (1999). Effects of Peruvian maca on hormonal functions. In *Medical Journal Report of Innovative Biologics.* (Reprinted from *Townsend Letter to Doctors and Patients, 184* (1998).) Retrieved September 15, 2001, from http://www.wholeworldbotanicals.com /journal.html

Wong, W. (n. d.). *Increasing fertility and maintaining pregnancy naturally.* Retrieved June 11, 2006, from www.totalityofbeing.com

Zheng, B. L., He, K., Kim, C. H., Rogers, L., Shao, R. V., Huang, Z. Y., et al. (2000). Effect of a lipid extract from Lepidium meyenii on sexual behavior in mice and rats. *Urology,* 55, 598-602.